'Here is a book that not c
consider lament as part
actually helps you pray t
It provides a broader context for lament within tne
witness of the Bible.'

- *Federico G. Villanueva, author, 'It's OK to be not
OK: Preaching the Lament Psalms,' and Scholar
Care Coordinator in Asia for Langham
Partnership, uk.langham.org*

'This is a gem of a book born out of prayerful
reflection on painful experience and careful
consideration of the words of Scripture. With
clarity and sensitivity, David serves up bitesize
chunks to nourish our understanding and fuel our
practice of lament.'

- *Dr. Paul Coulter, Head of Ministry Operations,
Living Leadership, Executive Director, Centre for
Christianity in Society, www.paulcoulter.net*

'Pain just happens. Life, as imperfect as it is right now, can bring us to our knees. This book uses Lament as a Biblical and thoroughly practical guide through our grief. David is experienced both as a Bible teacher and human who has grieved, and is a wise guide in the dark days of pain. I comment this book to you.'

*- Revd. Sara-Jane Stevens, pastor, priest and fellow grief-carrier*

'Discovering Lament is a solidly biblical study of this often-neglected element of Christian spirituality.'

*- Douglas Groothuis, Distinguished University Research Professor of Apologetics and Christian Worldview, Cornerstone University; author, 'Walking Through Twilight,'*
*www.DouglasGroothuis.com*

'When you face overwhelming sorrow and loss, this book will help you to bring your grief to God in a way that is honest, realistic, and above all, biblical. It contains a month of daily scriptural reflections and prayers brimming over with hope for the dark places on life's journey.'

*- Mike Licona, Professor of New Testament Studies at Houston Christian University; President of Risen Jesus, Inc., www.risenjesus.com*

'A fallen world can be full of pain and grief. How are we to be honest about that before God? In a series of short but significant reflections on lament, David Couchman walks us through how to handle pain and bring it to God with a heart where faith seeks understanding. There is much to learn through reading this book.'

*- Darrell L. Bock, Executive Director for Cultural Engagement, Howard G Hendricks Center for Christian Leadership and Cultural Engagement; Senior Research Professor of New Testament Studies, Dallas Theological Seminary, www.dts.edu*

'How do we handle those times when life throws up a clash between our belief in God's goodness and our everyday lived experience? In *Discovering Lament*, David Couchman has written a superb guide to help those wrestling with pain, loss, grief, or sadness. Deeply biblical, pastorally sensitive, and incredibly practical, *Discovering Lament* helps the reader bring their emotions honestly to the Lord - and also discover the light and hope that is shed upon them by the life, death, and resurrection of Jesus, the suffering saviour and man of sorrows. Whether you're experiencing trauma and pain yourself and are looking for comfort, or you're seeking to help somebody who is, *Discovering Lament* is a wonderfully rich collection of readings, reflections, and prayers.'

*- Dr. Andy Bannister, Director, Solas Centre for Public Christianity,* www.solas-cpc.org

'In this book David takes us by the hand and leads us to places where we can gaze on scripture landscapes we may never have taken seriously before, but then, perhaps we never needed them before like we do now. Lament is the resource you hope never to need, and then find so helpful when troubles and trials come. It reminds us that it is okay to be real, honest and open before God. This short set of readings, quotations and prayers will enrich your soul and strengthen your faith. I commend it warmly.'

*- Revd Dr Eric Gaudion, Author, Retired Pastor & Missionary, www.ericgaudion.blogspot.com*

'Life can be hard. Our plans shattered by a tragedy, sickness or loss. For many of us this will be disorientating and leave us at a loss for words. Perhaps sometimes we forget that for the writers of the Bible this is familiar territory. Drawing upon the Book of Lamentations, David Couchman provides a profound but simple guide to this difficult terrain. Divided into brief, insightful chapters, including model prayers, which make for perfect devotional studies. Theologically astute, pastorally sensitive, and always accessible, this book feels less like you are being told something and more like you are being shown something.  Avoiding simple cliches, David enables us to rediscover the language of lament and find light and hope in the darkest of times.'

*- Dr. Chris Sinkinson, Associate Minister, Lansdowne Church, Bournemouth UK, www.lansdownechurch.uk*

'In drawing deeply from both his own personal experience and his honest wrestling with the text of the Bible, David has served the church, and especially those in the midst of the darkest valleys, well. These 31 days of devotionals and ideas for prayer, would make an ideal 'pastoral accompaniment' for any who are struggling. There are no easy answers here though, but rather a grappling with the mystery and depths of suffering in the Scriptures and yet still pointing us to the certainty of the hope that we have.'

*- Revd. Dan Steel, Ministry Program Director, Lanier Theological Library and Learning Centre, Yarnton Manor, Oxford; author, Wise Church Planting, yarntonmanor.org*

# Discovering

# Lament

# Discovering

# Lament

## Bringing our grief to God

David A. Couchman

ISBN: 978-1-0686226-0-1

Copyright © David A Couchman 2024
*david@couchman.me.uk*

# Contents

# Introduction

Our first grandchild, Miriam, was born in 2013, and she was severely disabled. She could not feed and had to be fed through a tube.

As Mim grew, it became evident that she could not do any of the things healthy babies and toddlers can: she could not hold things, she could not sit, or stand, or walk, or talk. She was as severely disabled as it is possible to be, and the whole family loved her to bits.

Eventually, we found out that Mim had a very rare genetic condition. At the time, fewer than a dozen people in the world were known to have this condition. She truly was one in a billion.

A couple of years after Mim was born, Judy and I left Hampshire, where I had lived for more than forty years, and moved to Oxfordshire to help our daughter Hannah and son-in-law Jon look after Mim.

And then, two and a half years later, Mim died in the night. Her death came out of the blue. It was completely unexpected, and our family was devastated. Over the years since then, I have spent a lot of time reading and thinking and praying about loss and grief, and trying to understand what the Bible really says about it. This book is the result of that reading and praying.

It is divided into 31 short chapters, so that you can read one chapter a day for a month – although of course it does not have to be read like that.

Each chapter includes a Bible reading and a short reflection followed by some questions, intended to help you think through how the material relates to your own situation. The section concludes with a short prayer. This is only there as a suggestion, to help if you are struggling to find the words. Please feel free to ignore it and to pray in your own words.

# Getting started

# 1. A world of grief

## The Bible

Read Psalm 10:1-18

*Why, Lord, do you stand far off? Why do you hide yourself in times of trouble? (v1)*

We cannot avoid the reality of grief. We live in a sad and sorry world, a world messed up by sin and stupidity and suffering. There will always be distress caused by the evil actions of people, such as wars and pollution. The writer of Psalm 10 talks about the wicked man who hunts down the weak (v2).

Then there are natural disasters – epidemics, earthquakes, floods, and famines. These are not caused by wicked people – or at least, not directly. They seem to 'just happen', without rhyme or reason.

Our personal worlds are also torn by griefs – the breakdown of our relationships, serious illnesses, and losing people who matter to us.

For the follower of Jesus Christ, grief is often made worse when it seems as if God is so distant and silent. We are bombarded by doubts and questions, fears and anxieties.

We need to discover how to handle our grief well – how to lament.

## To think about

- What situations in the wider world are causing grief and distress at the moment?
- What situations in the lives of the people I know are causing them grief and distress?
- What situations in my own life are causing me grief and distress?

## A prayer

Dear loving Father in Heaven, thank you that you know about the things in the world around me, in the lives of people I know, and in my own life that are causing distress and grief. I ask that you will help me learn to handle my grief well. I pray this in the name of my Lord and Saviour, Jesus Christ. Amen.

## 2. What is lament?

### The Bible

Read Psalm 6:1-10

*My soul is in deep anguish. How long, Lord, how long?*

*Turn, Lord, and deliver me; save me because of your unfailing love.* (v3-4)

To *lament* means to express our grief and distress. Traditionally, British people – and many others – are brought up *not* to express our grief, to have a 'stiff upper lip'. Lament is the opposite of this. It is expressing our grief.

For the follower of Jesus Christ, to lament means to express our grief and distress *to God*. It may include *complaining* to God, or *questioning* God about our situation: 'Why, O Lord?' – Why this? Why me? Why now? 'How long, O Lord?' and 'Where are you, O Lord?'

For the follower of Jesus Christ, lament grows out of the tension between what we believe (that God is good) and what we experience in our lives (pain and loss). If we did not experience the loss and pain, we would not need to lament, and if we did not believe that God is good, there would be no point in lamenting.

As Mark Vroegop says, '*Lament is the honest cry of a hurting heart wrestling with the paradox of pain and the promise of God's goodness.*'[1]

We may think it is wrong to complain to God or to question God like this. However, the Bible includes a lot of lament. It seems that God can take it, and God wants us to bring our grief and distress to him.

## To think about

- What is it in my life that drives me to lament?
- What do I most want to say to God or ask God about it?

## A prayer

Dear loving Father in Heaven, thank you that you know how I feel, and that the Bible includes the words of people who felt the same. I ask that you help me to keep bringing my grief and distress to you. I pray this in the name of my Lord and Saviour, Jesus Christ. Amen.

*'Such radically inexplicable disasters fill biblical believers with desperate, passionate concern for the very nature of God. So they cry out in vertigo above the chasm that seems to gape between the God they know and the world they live in. If God is supposed to be like that, how can the world be like this? ... Lament is the voice of faith struggling to live with unanswered questions and unexplained suffering.'[2]*

- Christopher Wright

# 3. Why we need to discover lament

## The Bible

Read Psalm 61:1-8

*Hear my cry, O God; listen to my prayer. From the ends of the earth I call to you, I call as my heart grows faint; lead me to the rock that is higher than I.* (v1-2)

One reason we need to discover how to lament today is that our Christian experiences – for example the songs we sing, the sermons we listen to, and the books we read – have not equipped us to handle our grief well.

It can sometimes seem as if there is no place in our churches for people who are suffering loss, grief, and pain – for us to acknowledge what we are feeling and how it is affecting us spiritually, emotionally, mentally, and even physically.

It is almost as if we think it is sinful to complain to God or to question God's ways.

There is a kind of thinking that wants to brush off our sorrows. As if to say, 'Yes, you are going through a rotten time, but deep down everything is really wonderful, isn't it?' And the honest answer would be, 'No. It isn't wonderful at all. It's miserable. And just throwing out-of-context Bible verses at it and encouraging me to sing praise songs seems pretty vacuous.'

The church sometimes encourages a kind of dishonesty in those who are grieving. It wants us to plaster a smile on our faces and say that everything is all right – even when our hearts are breaking.

And yet... and yet... there is a huge amount about lament in the Bible. The 'go-to' places in the Old Testament are the book of Job and the Psalms. There is even a whole book called *Lamentations*. When did you last hear anyone preach a sermon from it?

Lament is there in the Bible, but missing from our Christian experience, and there is no room for it in our churches. Something has gone wrong.

## To think about

- How has my Christian experience prepared me to handle grief well?
- How could it have prepared me better?

## A prayer

Dear loving Father in Heaven, thank you that there are words of lament in the Bible, even if my Christian experience has not prepared me for it, and the church does not know how to handle it. I ask that you will help me discover how to lament well. Help us together as your people to respond more helpfully to one other when we face grief and distress. I pray this in the name of my Lord and Saviour, Jesus Christ. Amen.

*'I feel that the language of lament is seriously neglected in the church. Many Christians seem to feel that somehow it can't be right to complain to God in the context of corporate worship when we should all feel happy. There is an implicit pressure to stifle our real feelings because we are urged, by pious merchants of emotional denial, that we ought to have 'faith' (as if the moaning psalmists didn't). So we end up giving external voice to pretended emotions we do not really feel, while hiding the real emotions we are struggling with deep inside. Going to worship can become an exercise in pretence and concealment, neither of which can possibly be conducive for a real encounter with God.'*[3]

- Christopher Wright

# 4. Be honest with yourself

## The Bible

*Behold, you delight in truth in the inward being, and you teach me wisdom in the secret heart.* (Psalm 51:6, English Standard Version)

*Above all else, guard your heart, for everything you do flows from it.* (Proverbs 4:23)

So how do we discover lament? The vital first step is to be honest with ourselves about how we are feeling: not to pretend to ourselves that everything is fine, when really it is not; to recognise that there is not going to be a quick fix; and to admit that 'it's OK to be not OK' (as Federico Villanueva says[4]). Being honest with ourselves is not the whole story, but we cannot make any progress without it.

At a practical level, many people have found it helpful to record how they are feeling in a daily journal or diary.

Then we need to learn to be realistic with ourselves. This may mean dialling back our expectations of what we can do. Many of the people around us will also have expectations of us. We do not have to fulfil all these expectations.

A word of caution is needed here. It is right to cut yourself some slack when you are grieving and distressed – but this is not the time to dial back on your relationship with God. (We will come back to this.) This is not the time to lose your grip morally, or to compromise with sin.

## To think about

- Am I being honest with myself about how I think and feel?
- Am I being realistic in my expectations of myself?
- Am I being driven by other people's expectations of me?

## A prayer

Dear loving Father in Heaven, thank you that you always know how I am really feeling. I ask that you will help me to be honest with myself about how I feel, to be realistic in what I expect of myself, and not to be driven by what other people expect of me. I pray this in the name of my Lord and Saviour, Jesus Christ. Amen.

# 5. The most important thing

## The Bible

Read Psalm 142:1-7

*I cry aloud to the Lord; I lift up my voice to the Lord for mercy.*

*I pour out before him my complaint; before him I tell my trouble...*

*I cry to you, Lord, I say, 'You are my refuge, my portion in the land of the living. Listen to my cry, for I am in desperate need...'* (v1-2, 5-6)

When we are going through grief and distress it can often feel as though God is not listening. We may start to wonder whether we are really his people, or whether he is really good, or whether he is really there. Our hearts quickly fill with questions and doubts and fears, and we may even be angry with God.

When we feel like this, the temptation is to stop talking to God about it – to think that there is no point. How will it help?

However, the most important single thing we can do when we are going through grief and distress is to keep talking to God about it.

Nothing is more important than continuing to talk to God, but how do we go about it? We do not know what to say! We do not even know where to start. We will explore these questions next.

## To think about

- How do I feel about praying?
- What tempts me to give up?
- What helps me to keep going?

## A prayer

Dear loving Father in Heaven, thank you that you know how I feel. You know about my questions, my doubts, my fears, and my anxieties. I ask that you will help me to keep bringing them to you, even when I do not feel like it. I pray this in the name of my Lord and Saviour, Jesus Christ. Amen.

*'Above all, keep close to the throne of grace. If we seem to get no good by attempting to draw near to him, we may be sure we shall get none by keeping away from him.'*[5]

- John Newton

# Getting started – what have we discovered?

To lament means to express our grief and distress. For the follower of Jesus Christ, it means expressing our grief and distress *to God*. This may include complaining to God and asking God questions about what is happening.

Lament grows out of the tension between believing that God is good and experiencing pain and loss. There is a lot of lament in the Bible, but we are not familiar with it today, which is why we need to discover how to lament – to bring our grief to God.

Lament begins with being honest with ourselves about what we are feeling, and talking to God about it.

# Bringing our grief to God

# 6. Be honest with God

## The Bible

Read Jeremiah 20:7-12

*You deceived me, and I was deceived.* (v7)


When we are going through grief and distress, we need to be honest with ourselves about how we feel, and we need to keep talking to God, even when we do not feel like it. It is vitally important to be honest with God – to tell him what we *really* think and feel, not what we *ought to* think and feel.


Being honest with God is hard. We instinctively believe we have to feel and think a certain way before we can come to God. If we do not feel that way, we must put on an act. *Surely God would not want to hear what I really have to say,* we might think. This is not so! The Bible is full of examples of people who come to God honestly – and God does not condemn them.

One of the most extreme examples is Jeremiah. God has called Jeremiah to be a prophet, but the people refuse to listen to his message, and indeed they turn against him. In Jeremiah 20, he complains bitterly to God.

When Jeremiah realises that his calling is bringing him suffering and grief, he cries out, '*You deceived me, and I was deceived.*' (Jeremiah 20:7) God has not really deceived Jeremiah – he has never promised Jeremiah that he will succeed. But that is how Jeremiah feels, and he brings it honestly to God.

In 1 Kings 18 and 19, after Elijah's great victory over the priests of Baal, the evil queen Jezebel threatens to kill him, and he runs away. Worn out and exhausted physically and emotionally, he says to God, '*Please take away my life. I'm no better than my ancestors.*' (1 Kings 19:4)

After Job has lost everything, he curses the day he was born (Job 3:1).

You can probably think of other examples too. People in the Bible were honest with God about how they felt – and God did not condemn them for it. God wants us to be honest with him.

We do need to be careful here: In the book of Job, when Job was going through all kinds of suffering, it says that '*Job did not sin by charging God with wrongdoing*' (Job 1:22). It would have been wrong for Job to blame God for what had happened to him, and it would be wrong for us too. However, the basic point remains: it is better to be honest about being in the wrong place than to pretend to be in the right place.

We will look next at some resources in the Bible that help us to be honest with God.

## To think about

- How do I feel about my life right now?
- Can I talk to God honestly about how I feel? If not, why not?

## A prayer

Dear loving Father in Heaven, thank you that you want me to be honest with you about how I feel and that you can handle it. Please help me to bring my feelings to you sincerely. I pray this in the name of my Lord and Saviour, Jesus Christ. Amen.

# 7. Songs of Sorrow

## The Bible

Read Psalm 13:1-6

*Look on me and answer, Lord my God.* (v3)

We need to discover how to lament today because of all the grief in our lives, and because our Christian experience often has not equipped us to handle grief well. However, lament is in the Bible.

As we begin to discover how to lament, we will find that the Bible gives us many helpful resources. Some of these are found in the book of Psalms: about one in three psalms are laments. They are basically complaints to God. Yet they are still in the Bible! Not only that; they are in Israel's hymn book. They are the nation of Israel's songs of sorrow.

Some of the psalms are *individual* laments – they are the words of a single person caught up in distress and grief. Some are *communal* laments – they express the grief and distress of the whole

33

nation or community. We will look at the psalms of communal lament later.

A lot of the lament psalms have the same basic shape:

- A complaint or question to God
- Asking God for help
- Expressing trust in God

Psalm 13 is an example of lament:

- A complaint or question – verses 1-2: '*How long O Lord? Will you forget me for ever?*'
- Asking God for help – verses 3-4: '*Look on me and answer, O Lord my God...*'
- Expressing trust in God – verses 5-6: '*But I trust in your unfailing love...*'

The lament psalms do two important things:

- They give us permission to be honest with God. They are in the Bible. God lets his people speak honestly to him when we are in distress and grief. In fact, he *wants* us to be honest with him.

- They also give us words to use when we cannot find words of our own. That is one reason why praying through the lament psalms can be helpful. We can pray them to God as they stand, or we can follow their basic shape of complaint/asking/trusting in our own prayers.

Some psalms of individual lament: Psalm 3, 5, 7, 17, 22, 25, 26, 28, 38, 39, 42-43, 54, 55, 56, 57, 59, 63, 64, 69, 70, 71, 77, 86, 120, 140, 141, 142, 143.

## To think about

- What do I most want to say to God right now?
- How does Psalm 13 help me say it?

## A prayer

Dear loving Father in Heaven, thank you that the psalms of lament give me permission to be honest with you and give me words to use when I cannot find words of my own. Please help me to bring my complaints honestly to you, to ask for your help, and to keep trusting you. I pray this in the name of my Lord and Saviour, Jesus Christ. Amen.

'*It surely cannot be accidental that in the divinely inspired book of Psalms there are more psalms of lament and anguish than of joy and thanksgiving. These are words that God has actually given to us. God has allowed them a prominent place in his authorized songbook. We need both forms of worship in abundance as we live in this wonderful, terrible world.*'[6]

- Christopher Wright

# 8. When darkness is my closest friend

## The Bible

Read Psalm 88:1-18

*You have taken from me friend and neighbour – darkness is my closest friend.* (v18)

In most of the lament psalms, the writer ends by expressing his trust in God. Most. But not all. Psalm 88 begins with the writer crying out to God and ends with him saying that the darkness is his closest friend.

There is no 'happy ending' in this Psalm. The author ends up alone in the darkness. Yet this Psalm is still in the Bible. That is something to think about.

This says to us not only that God wants us to be honest with him, but also that when we *are* honest with him, this does not mean we shall always end up in a place of peace and trust – or at least, not any time soon. Sometimes the darkness is still our closest friend.

And yet... and yet... On the cross, Jesus cried out, '*My God, my God, why have you forsaken me?*' He endured the darkness for us. Because of this, we can know that God will never really abandon us, however much we feel alone in the darkness.

## To think about

- Where am I right now? Am I trusting God? Or am I still in the place where darkness is my closest friend?
- How could I use Psalm 88 or one of the other lament psalms in my own praying to help me be honest with God?

## A prayer

Dear loving Father in Heaven, thank you that even when I feel that the darkness is my closest friend, you are still there, and you still care. I ask that you will help me know that even in the darkness, you are with me. I pray this in the name of my Lord and Saviour, Jesus Christ. Amen.

*'Psalm 88 is the saddest, darkest, bleakest psalm in the Bible. Other psalms express agony and heart-wrenching sorrow, but all of them end with trust and hope. Psalm 88 is different. It ends in darkness, with the absence of God.*

*'These aren't verses to display on our fridge door or kitchen noticeboard. These aren't verses to write out over a backdrop of a sunrise or waterfall and share on social media. These are the prayers and thoughts we keep hidden – locked away. They would be repulsive to our altogether 'sorted' and believing friends. Perhaps our prayer*

*is not so much 'help my unbelief' as 'hide my unbelief'.*

*'The Bible never whitewashes our pain and sorrow. Psalm 88 doesn't need to be explained away. It is the heartfelt expression of a genuine believer, just as much as the loud songs of praise are. This psalm isn't hidden away in an appendix, or hushed up so as not to 'let the side down'. This prayer is in the heart of Scripture, approved by God. It's not the normal expectation of life as a believer. But how encouraging it is to know that it is possible to speak like this and still be a believer.'[7]*

- Matt Searles

# 9. No comfort

## The Bible

Read Lamentations 1:1-11

*Her fall was astounding; there was none to comfort her.*

*Look, Lord, on my affliction, for the enemy has triumphed.* (v9)

In 587 BC, the Babylonian Empire conquered Jerusalem. The fall of the city is a vitally important event, described four times in the Bible – in 2 Kings 25, 2 Chronicles 36, Jeremiah 39, and Jeremiah 52. Many of the people were taken away into captivity in Babylon. The city was destroyed, and the Temple was burned down. More than just a building, this was the place where people could meet with God. It was the heart of Jewish worship.

Lamentations is a collection of five songs bewailing the fall of Jerusalem. The survivors who were left in the city probably gathered in the ruins of the Temple to sing these songs.

The people of Judah and Jerusalem had lost something precious, which they could never get back. One of the central themes of Lamentations is grief for irretrievable loss.

Chapter 1 is a lament for the desolate city. The key theme is that there is 'no comfort' for the city or its people (repeated in verses 2, 9, 16, 17, and 21).

Lamentations 1 is divided into two parts. In verses 1-11, the city is described in the third person ('*How like a widow is she...*' v1). In verses 12-22, the city speaks in the first person ('*Is any suffering like my suffering...*' v12).

More than two thousand years later, we do not live in the ruins of Jerusalem. However, for many of us, there is someone in our past whom we have lost and for whom we grieve, or something we have lost and for which we grieve.

We can be encouraged that the Bible does not brush loss and grief under the carpet. It does not say, 'Oh, that isn't appropriate for a believer.' Rather, it includes the full range of human experience, including grief and loss.

There are some hints in the way Lamentations is organised that help us understand its message. However, these hints are not particularly obvious in English translations. You may find it helpful to look at the appendix on 'How is *Lamentations* organised?'

## To think about

- What is the same in my situation and Lamentations? (Irretrievable loss? No comfort? Something else?)
- What is different?

## A prayer

Dear loving Father in Heaven, thank you that your Word includes the book of Lamentations, with all its loss and grief. I ask that as I read it, you will speak to me through these ancient words. I pray this in the name of my Lord and Saviour, Jesus Christ. Amen.

*'The 'earthy' and real experience of tragedy in life is a note rung in the symphony of Scripture, and this reality should reverberate in modern faith – the Bible is not always praise-oriented. Nor does it put a naïve, happy face on pain. Rather, Scripture shows tragedy in all of its mournful detail.'*[8]

- Heath Thomas

# 10. We do not know why

## The Bible

Read Lamentations 1:12-22

*The Lord is righteous, yet I rebelled against his command...*

*See, Lord, how distressed I am! I am in torment within, and in my heart I am disturbed, for I have been most rebellious... (v18-20)*

The desolation of Jerusalem was God's punishment on the people for their sins of idolatry, immorality, and injustice. This is mentioned several times in chapter 1 (verses 5, 8, 14, 18, and 22) and is shown in more length in chapter 2. For centuries before God's judgement fell, he had warned his people through the prophets.

Sometimes, suffering and grief are the result of our sin – either a direct consequence, or as God's judgment. Sometimes, but not always. Think of Job. His sufferings were not a result of his sin – Job suffered precisely because he was faithful to God. (Job 1:8)

Think of the man born blind, in John 9. When Jesus's followers asked him, '*Who sinned, this man or his parents, that he was born blind?*' (v2) Jesus's reply was, '*Neither this man nor his parents sinned, but this happened so that the works of God might be displayed in him.*' (v3)

When we are 'going through it', we need to be very careful not to jump to the conclusion that God is punishing us. We live in a fallen, damaged world, and we cannot usually see any *direct* connection between suffering and sin. More often than not, we simply do not know why some particular grief has come our way, and we have to accept that we do not know. Someone once said that the useful question to ask is not 'Why?' but 'What?' – 'What does God want me to learn through this experience?'

What we do know is that if we trust Christ, there is no condemnation for us, and all our sins have been forgiven. (Romans 8:1)

This means that we need to be careful how we read Lamentations. Some of what it says may not apply directly to us. We can still use it, and we can still find it helpful – but we need to take care how we read it.

## To think about

- What could God want me to learn through what has happened, or is happening, in my life?

## A prayer

Dear loving Father in Heaven, thank you that you know all about the distress in my heart, and the muddle and confusion in my mind when I think about what is happening. Please help me not to jump to wrong conclusions about you. Help me to trust you when I do not understand, and to turn to you rather than turning away from you. Help me to learn what you want me to learn. I pray this in the name of my Lord and Saviour, Jesus Christ. Amen.

# 11. Praying our pain

## The Bible

Read Lamentations 2:18-22

*Look, Lord, and consider: whom have you ever treated like this? ... Young and old lie together in the dust of the streets; my young men and young women have fallen by the sword. You have slain them in the day of your anger; you have slaughtered them without pity.* (v20-21)

The desolation that has fallen on Jerusalem (Lamentations 1) is not just an accident of history. It is a result of the people's sin and God's judgment. Lamentations 2:1-10 is all about what God has done because of his anger with his people's sin. Verses 11-17 describe the people's grief. How should they respond to God's judgment? By praying. Verses 18-19 are a call to prayer, and verses 20-22 are a prayer.

When we suffer grief and loss, we are always tempted to turn away from God – to think that he is not there, or if he is there, that he does not care.

Lamentations reminds us how important it is to turn *to* God, and to bring our loss and grief and distress to him. We need to keep reminding ourselves that God really is there, and that we matter to him. As 1 Peter 5:7 says: 'Cast all your anxiety on him because he cares for you.'

Lamentations includes both grief over loss, and prayer in this grief: its central theme is 'praying our pain'.

## To think about

- What do I most struggle with about praying my pain?
- How does Lamentations help me to pray my pain?

## A prayer

Dear loving Father in Heaven, thank you that you really are there, and that what happens to me matters very much to you. Please help me not to turn away from you, but to bring my sorrow and grief and pain to you. I pray this in the name of my Lord and Saviour, Jesus Christ. Amen.

# 12. There is hope

## The Bible

Read Lamentations 3:21-33

*Because of the Lord's great love we are not consumed, for his compassions never fail. They are new every morning; great is your faithfulness. I say to myself, 'The Lord is my portion; therefore I will wait for him.' (v22-24)*

Chapter 3 is not just the centre of the book of Lamentations; it is the centre of the message of Lamentations. The heart of chapter 3 is the heart of its message. (See the appendix on 'How is *Lamentations* organised?')

Chapter 3 begins with a personal lament, in verses 1-20 – God has become my enemy! Then there is a sudden and completely unexpected pivot at verse 21, which goes on through to verse 39.

The key word in these verses is 'hope':

'*Yet this I call to mind and therefore I have hope...*' (v21)

'*The Lord is good to those whose hope is in him, to the one who seeks him...*' (v25)

'*Let him sit alone in silence, for the Lord has laid it on him. Let him bury his face in the dust – there may yet be hope.*' (v29)

The English Standard Version also translates verse 24 as: "*The Lord is my portion,' says my soul, 'therefore I will hope in him.*"

These verses are the key message of Lamentations. It is easy to read them as being wonderfully positive and encouraging (and they are). However, we need to remember that the situation has not changed. Jerusalem has been destroyed! The city is still in ruins, and the people are still grieving. Yet – in spite of all this – God is faithful. Because of his great love, he has not let us be completely destroyed. We are still here! Because of this, there is hope.

## To think about

- How can I affirm God's love and faithfulness *in the middle of* my distress and grief?
- What difference does this make to me?

## A prayer

Dear loving Father in Heaven, thank you for your great love for us, which will not let us be completely destroyed. Thank you for your compassion that never fails and is new every morning. Thank you for your great faithfulness, even in the middle of grief and loss and suffering. Thank you that you do not cast us off for ever. Thank you that you do not willingly bring affliction or grief to anyone. Please help me to put my hope in you and to seek you. I pray this in the name of my Lord and Saviour, Jesus Christ. Amen.

# 13. Waiting for God

## The Bible

Read Lamentations 3:24-33

*I say to myself, 'The Lord is my portion; therefore I will wait for him. The Lord is good to those whose hope is in him, to the one who seeks him; it is good to wait quietly for the salvation of the Lord. It is good for a man to bear the yoke while he is young.'* (v24-27)

We have seen that Lamentations 3:22-33 is at the heart of the message of Lamentations. The key is the sudden pivot at verse 21-22: '*Because of the Lord's great love we are not consumed...*' (in spite of the havoc and desolation all around).

We have also seen that the key word in these verses is 'hope' (verses 21, 25, and 29). But there is another important word in these verses – the word 'wait' – *waiting* for God to act:

'*The Lord is my portion; therefore I will wait for him...*

*it is good to wait quietly for the salvation of the Lord.*'
(Lamentations 3:24, 26)

The same theme is drawn out in verse 31, although the word 'wait' itself is not used: '*For no one is cast off by the Lord for ever.*'

There is a very close relationship between hoping and waiting. Verse 21 (*therefore I have hope*) and verse 24 (*therefore I will wait*) are actually the same phrase in the original Hebrew. In the New Testament, Paul picks up this idea in Romans 8:25, when he says, '*If we hope for what we do not yet have, we wait for it patiently.*'

This brings us back to one of the key questions of lament: 'How long, O Lord...?' How long must I wait for you to do something?

Sometimes God seems to take a long time to intervene. His timescale is different from ours.

Waiting changes us, and it brings to light what we really believe about God and how we feel towards him. Part of discovering lament is learning to wait well for God to act in his time.

'*Wait for the Lord; be strong and take heart and wait for the Lord.*' (Psalm 27:14)

## To think about

- How do I handle it when life is tragic and it feels as if God is not doing anything?
- When I am kept waiting, what does this reveal about what I believe about God and how I feel towards him?
- How is waiting changing me?

## A prayer

Dear loving Father in Heaven, thank you that you are in control of my life, and that your timing is always right, even when it does not feel like it. Thank you that you know how I think and feel when it seems you are not doing anything. Please help me to trust you, and to wait patiently for you to act. I pray this in the name of my Lord and Saviour, Jesus Christ. Amen.

*'Do you find it easy to wait? Most of us don't because waiting does something to us...*

*'Waiting also tells us something. It shows what our relationship is to the person or the event we are waiting for. Would a man wait for his fiancée in the same way he waits for his income tax bill? If he did, it might not tell us much about his fiancée. But it would tell us volumes about his opinion of her...*

*'Waiting does something to us, and it tells us something about our relationship to God.'* [9]

- Os Guinness

# 14. The pain is still there

## The Bible

Read Lamentations 4:1-22

*Your punishment will end, Daughter Zion;*
*he will not prolong your exile.*
*But he will punish your sin, Daughter Edom,*
*and expose your wickedness.* (v22)

If we had been writing Lamentations, we might have thought that chapter 3 was a good place to stop: '*Because of the Lord's great love we are not consumed, for his compassions never fail. They are new every morning; great is your faithfulness.*' (3:22)

However, the situation has not changed! Yes, God is indeed loving and compassionate and faithful – but the suffering and distress are still real and still present. The city has still been destroyed, and the people are still devastated. So chapter 4 begins with another lament in verses 1-11, remembering what Jerusalem was, and contrasting that with what it is now. Verses 12-16 acknowledge again that this has happened because of the sins of the people, and particularly because of the sins of the leaders – the priests and prophets. Verses 17-20 describe some of the vain hopes of the people – the allies they had relied on who had let them down. However, after this, verses 21-22 sound a note of genuine hope: God's judgment on Jerusalem will not last for ever. One day, it will come to an end – but the enemies who have laughed over Jerusalem's destruction will themselves be judged too.

This brings us back to the key theme of Lamentations – praying our pain. The pain is still there. God is still there too, and he is faithful. Lamentations is about bringing our pain to our faithful God in prayer.

And yet... chapter 4 is the only chapter in Lamentations that does not include any explicit prayer. It is as if, after the high point of chapter 3, the writer is saying, 'Don't forget the present reality.'

## To think about

- How does reflecting on God's love and compassion and faithfulness change how I feel about my pain?
- How does my pain change how I understand God's love and compassion and faithfulness?
- What does it mean, in practice, for me to bring my pain to God in prayer?

## A prayer

Dear loving Father in Heaven, thank you that you are still loving and compassionate and faithful, even in the middle of tragedy and loss and grief. Please help me to keep holding on to you, and to keep bringing my pain to you. I pray this in the name of my Lord and Saviour, Jesus Christ. Amen.

# 15. Remember, restore, and renew!

## The Bible

Read Lamentations 5:1-22

*Restore us to yourself, O Lord, that we may return; renew our days as of old, unless you have utterly rejected us and are angry with us beyond measure.* (v19-22)

As if to make up for the lack of prayer in chapter 4, the whole of chapter 5 is a prayer. The key word in verse 1 is 'remember' – *'Remember, O Lord,'* followed in verses 2-18 by another long lament and a final prayer in verses 19-22: *'Restore us to yourself, O Lord...'*

The book of Lamentations is deeply ambiguous. Perhaps this is one reason why we do not hear many sermons on it: most of us do not handle ambiguity well, and we do not think our faith should be uncertain. Things should be clear cut.

A central theme that comes out again and again is God's anger with his people because of their sins (2:1-9; 4:11). Yet God's unfailing love, mercy, and compassion are also key themes (3:22-33).

Is this ambiguity just an accident? Is it because Lamentations is poorly thought out? No. The ambiguity is deliberate – it reflects the way real life is deeply ambiguous. We believe that God loves us and cares for us, and yet we face all kinds of tragedies. As we said at the start of these reflections, lament grows out of this tension between what we believe about the goodness of God (Lamentations 3:21-25) and the pain and loss we experience (Lamentations 5). This ambiguity will not be completely resolved this side of the new creation.

The book of Lamentations ends with a question – the ambiguity has not been resolved:

*'You, O Lord, reign forever; your throne endures from generation to generation. Why do you always forget us? Why do you forsake us so long? Restore*

*us to yourself, O Lord, that we may return; renew our days as of old unless you have utterly rejected us and are angry with us beyond measure.'* (Lamentations 5:19-22)

Real life often leaves us perplexed, full of questions and uncertainties, even while we affirm that God is good and loving. For more on the ambiguity of Lamentations see the appendix on 'How is *Lamentations* organised?'

## To think about

- How am I handling the tension between believing that God is good and experiencing loss and pain?
- How has exploring the book of Lamentations helped me to respond to this tension?

## A prayer

Dear loving Father in Heaven, thank you that I can come to you through Jesus Christ, in freedom and confidence, knowing that you have not rejected me but have made a way for me to come into your presence. Please remember what has happened to me. Please restore me to yourself. Please renew me, even in the middle of the ongoing tension and ambiguity of life. I ask this in the name of my Lord and Saviour, Jesus Christ. Amen.

*'Ultimately there are depths in God's actions that finite man cannot grasp. God's revelation in word and act consistently shows his justice and covenant love; yet there is always a residue of human experience that demands our bowing to a wisdom too high for our understanding.'*[10]

- H. L. Ellison

# Bringing our grief to God – what have we discovered?

When we are discovering lament, we need to be honest with God – to tell him what we really think and feel, not just what we believe we ought to think and feel.

People in the Bible were honest with God about how they felt – and God did not condemn them for it. God wants us to be honest with him.

We may feel we cannot find the words to speak honestly to God. This is where the Bible helps. Passages such as the lament psalms and the book of Lamentations do two things: they give us permission to be honest with God, and they give us words to use when we cannot find words of our own.

Lamentations, in particular, has a lot to teach us about praying our pain – about the ambiguity of life: the grief and loss are there, and they are real, and yet God is faithful and loving and merciful.

# Jesus and our griefs

# 16. 'A man of sorrows...'

## The Bible

Read Isaiah 53:1-6

*... A man of sorrows, acquainted with deepest grief.*
(v3, New Living Translation)

Today we are in a better place than the writers of Psalms and Lamentations were in Old Testament times, because we live this side of the life, death, and resurrection of Jesus. If we are followers of Christ, he is at the centre of everything we believe.

Because Jesus is a man, as well as the Son of God, he understands at first hand what it is like to grieve and to be distressed:

- He weeps at the grave of his friend Lazarus (John 11:35)
- He weeps over Jerusalem (Luke 19:41)
- He is deeply distressed in the Garden of Gethsemane (Matthew 26:38-39; Mark 14:33-34; Luke 22:44)

So Jesus knows what it is like.

## To think about

- What difference does it make to me that Jesus is a 'man of sorrows, acquainted with deepest grief' – that he knows at first hand what it is like to go through what I am going through?

## A prayer

Dear loving Father in Heaven, thank you that Jesus knows from experience what it is like to grieve and to be distressed. Thank you that he is 'a man of sorrows, acquainted with deepest grief'. I pray that when I am distressed and grieved, you will help me to remember that Jesus knows what it is like, and to bring my sorrows to you through him. I pray this in the name of my Lord and Saviour, Jesus Christ. Amen.

*'I could never myself believe in God, if it were not for the cross. The only God I could believe in is the One Nietzsche ridiculed as 'God on the cross'. In the real world of pain, how could one worship a God who was immune to it? I have entered many Buddhist temples in different Asian countries and stood respectfully before the statue of the Buddha, his legs crossed, arms folded, a remote look on his face, detached from the agonies of the world. But each time after a while I have had to turn away. And in imagination I have turned instead to that lonely, twisted, tortured figure on the cross, nails through hands and feet, back lacerated, limbs wrenched, brow bleeding from thorn-pricks, mouth dry and intolerably thirsty, plunged in God-forsaken darkness. That is the God for me! He laid aside his immunity to pain. He entered our world of flesh and blood, tears and death. Our sufferings become more manageable in the light of his. There is still a deep question mark against human suffering, but over it we boldly stamp another mark, the cross - which symbolises divine suffering.'*[11] - John Stott

# 17. He carried our sorrows

## The Bible

Read Isaiah 53:1-6

*Surely he took up our pain, and bore our suffering...* (v4)

We have reminded ourselves that Jesus knows what it is like. He has been through it. He is '*a man of sorrows, acquainted with deepest grief*'.

The Bible also says that he has carried our sorrows: '*... He took up our pain, and bore our suffering...*' (Isaiah 53:4)

This is talking first of all about Jesus carrying our sins. This is one of the foundation truths of the Christian message, and it is right for us to put it at the centre of our thinking. It is at the heart of the New Testament.

So, for example, Jesus said: '... *The Son of Man did not come to be served, but to serve, and to give his life as a ransom for many.*' (Mark 10:45)

And Paul says: '... *Christ died for our sins according to the Scriptures...*' (1 Corinthians 15:3)

However. the Bible also says that (in some way we do not fully understand) he carried our griefs. As the New Living Translation puts it: '*Yet it was our weaknesses he carried; it was our sorrows that weighed him down.*' (Isaiah 53:4)

## To think about

- What difference does it make to me that Jesus took up my weaknesses and carried my sorrows?

## A prayer

Dear loving Father in Heaven, thank you that Jesus carried my sorrows. Please help me not to try to carry them on my own. I pray this in the name of my Lord and Saviour, Jesus Christ. Amen.

# 18. Jesus is praying for you!

## The Bible

Read Romans 8:31-39; Hebrews 7:23-28

*Who then is the one who condemns? No one. Christ Jesus who died – more than that, who was raised to life – is at the right hand of God and is also interceding for us. Who shall separate us from the love of Christ? Shall trouble or hardship or persecution or famine or nakedness or danger or sword?* (Romans 8:34-35)

*... He is able to save completely those who come to God through him, because he always lives to intercede for them.* (Hebrews 7:25)

Jesus has lived our life. He walked our road. He knows what it is like to experience loss and grief and suffering. More than that, as Isaiah 53:4 says, he carried our sorrows.

However, Jesus is not just a figure from the past who knew what it was like to grieve, or who carried our sorrows then. He has been raised from the dead! He has overcome death and defeated all the spiritual powers ranged against us. Today, as Romans 8 and Hebrews 7 tell us, he is at his Father's side, praying for us.

Knowing that Jesus gets what it is like, that he has carried our griefs and sorrows, and that today he is in Heaven praying for us, can change how we pray. As the writer of Hebrews says, he is our great high priest who understands all our weaknesses:

*'For we do not have a high priest who is unable to feel sympathy for our weaknesses, but we have one who has been tempted in every way, just as we are – yet he did not sin. Let us then approach God's throne of grace with confidence, so that we may receive mercy and find grace to help us in our time of need.'* (Hebrews 4:15-16)

Or, as Paul says in Ephesians 3:12, '*In him and through faith in him, we can come to God with freedom and confidence.*' We can tell God freely what we are thinking and feeling, and we can be confident that he will hear us, because of Jesus.

As Mark Vroegop says, we can 'ask boldly because he understands deeply'.[12]

## To think about

- What difference does it make to me today that Jesus is in Heaven praying for me right now?

## A prayer

Dear loving Father in Heaven, thank you that Jesus is in your presence, in Heaven today, praying for me. Please help me to hold on to this truth, and to live in the light of it. I pray this in the name of my Lord and Saviour, Jesus Christ. Amen.

# Jesus and our griefs – what have we discovered?

Because of Jesus, we are in a better place than the writers of Psalms and Lamentations.

Because Jesus is a man, as well as the Son of God, he understands first-hand what it is like to grieve and to be distressed. He is '*a man of sorrows, acquainted with deepest grief*'. And '*He took up our pain, and bore our suffering.*' Now today he is in Heaven praying for us. And because of him, we can come to God as our loving Father in Heaven, and we can pray honestly to him with freedom and confidence.

# Attitudes

# 19. Look forward in hope

## The Bible

Read Revelation 21:1-8

*There will be no more death or mourning or crying or pain.* (v4)

We are looking next at some of the *attitudes* that are helpful for us to develop when we are lamenting. It will be useful to think about these in terms of attitudes to the *future*, the *past*, and the *present*.

As Revelation 21:4 says, there is a day coming when there will be no more death or mourning or crying or pain, because the present way things are arranged will have passed away. We need to become people who look forward to that day with hope. But this is not as simple as it sounds.

A pastor once asked his congregation, 'When are the good times?' When we think about the good times, do we think about the past, the present, or the future?

When we are going through grief and distress, the present can seem very bleak and dark, and the future very uncertain. We are easily tempted to live in the past – to dwell on our memories of when things were better, and to want to go back to the 'good old days'.

This is our natural inclination, but the Bible warns us: *'Don't long for 'the good old days.' This is not wise.'* (Ecclesiastes 7:10, New Living Translation)

For the follower of Jesus Christ, the real good times are in the future, not the past. One day, Jesus will return, and when he does, he will put right all the things that cause us so much grief and distress now.

As C. S. Lewis says, *'There are better things ahead than any we leave behind.'*[13]

So we need to develop an attitude of hope, looking forward to that day.

## To think about

- When I think of the good times, when do I think about?
- Am I looking back with regret, or forward with hope?
- What practical step can I take to develop an attitude of hope?

## A prayer

Dear loving Father in Heaven, thank you that there is a day coming when there will be no more death or mourning or crying or pain. Please help me to live these days in the light of that day. Help me not to look back to the 'good old days' but to look forward with hope. I pray this in the name of my Lord and Saviour, Jesus Christ. Amen.

*'Daydreaming and indulgence of nostalgia are unhappy habits, making for unrealism and discontent. Like all bad habits, they tighten their grip on us until we set ourselves against them and, with God's help, break them.'*[14]

- J. I. Packer

# 20. Grief and suffering will not last

## The Bible

Read 2 Corinthians 4:16-18

*... our light and momentary troubles are achieving for us an eternal glory that far outweighs them all.* (v17)

A key theme in the Bible is that our griefs and sufferings are only brief.

As Paul says in 2 Corinthians 4:17, our present troubles are *light and momentary* compared with the future glory that is both weighty and eternal.

In Hebrew thought, the glory of God was precisely his 'weightiness' – his solidity or substantiality. In 2 Corinthians 4, Paul draws a contrast between our present suffering and grief – which are insubstantial ('light') and brief ('momentary'), and the glory to come, which is substantial ('outweighs them all') and permanent ('eternal').

Of course, it is easy to say this, but when we are caught up in the middle of grief and suffering, they do not feel either brief or light. This leads into our next reflection.

## To think about

- What will help me remember that grief and suffering will not last long?

## A prayer

Dear loving Father in Heaven, thank you that my troubles really are only light and momentary when I look at them from the viewpoint of eternity. They are only for a little while, even if it does not feel like that when I am in the middle of them. Please help me to live with hope for the future, and in the present to live one day at a time, remembering that each day is a day nearer to my eternal home with you. I pray this in the name of my Lord and Saviour, Jesus Christ. Amen.

# 21. A choice to rejoice

## The Bible

Read 1 Peter 1:3-7

*Praise be to the God and Father of our Lord Jesus Christ! In his great mercy he has given us new birth into a living hope through the resurrection of Jesus Christ from the dead... In all this you greatly rejoice, though now for a little while you may have had to suffer grief in all kinds of trials.* (v3-6)

Peter talks here about the hope God has given us through Jesus being raised from the dead. Once again in these verses, we see the note that grief and trials are only brief – they are *'for a little while'*.

But Peter says something else here that is important: even in the middle of the griefs and trials, we can actually rejoice in our future hope.

As followers of Jesus Christ, we need to become people who look forward in hope. We also need to be realistic in what we hope for. Our hope is not that things will get better here and now. They may, or they may not. For the time being we may have to go on suffering grief. Our hope is for a future day in which we shall be with Christ, and all our suffering and grief will be ended. We can rejoice in this hope even while we are going through the trials.

But this kind of rejoicing does not come naturally to us. We have to make a deliberate choice to rejoice. Whenever we find ourselves looking back with nostalgia, and wanting to live in the past, we should choose to look forward in hope. We will look at this more closely later.

## To think about

- Am I looking forward in hope?
- Am I being realistic about what I hope for?
- What will help me make the choice to rejoice?

## A prayer

Dear loving Father in Heaven, thank you that in your great mercy you have given me new birth into a living hope, through the resurrection of Jesus. I ask you to help me to choose to look forward in hope. I pray this in the name of my Lord and Saviour, Jesus Christ. Amen.

# 22. Achieving an eternal glory

## The Bible

Read 2 Corinthians 4:16-18

*... our light and momentary troubles are achieving for us an eternal glory that far outweighs them all.* (v17)

We have thought about the coming day when there will be no more death or mourning or crying or pain. We have thought about the reality that our present grief and sufferings are only brief. We have also seen that we need to make a deliberate choice to rejoice, even in the middle of grief. Another important truth is that our present sufferings are actually *accomplishing* something. They are not just random, meaningless events, nor are they signs that God has turned against us. Rather, as Paul says here, they are *achieving for us* a glory that is weighty and eternal.

So how does this work in practice? It can feel like they are not achieving anything when we are going through them. They often seem completely pointless and meaningless.

In Romans 5:2-5, Paul says that we can rejoice in our future hope – yes, but more than that, '*We also rejoice in our sufferings, because we know that suffering produces perseverance; perseverance, character; and character, hope. And hope does not disappoint us, because God has poured out his love into our hearts by the Holy Spirit, whom he has given us.*'

We can not only rejoice in our future hope. There is even a sense in which we can rejoice in our present grief and sufferings. This seems like a tough call. When I look at the present, if I am honest, I do not always feel much like rejoicing.

It is not that we are somehow supposed to enjoy the grief and suffering in itself, but rather that we know it is achieving something for us. It is doing something to us – developing perseverance and character. It is making us ready for that eternal, weighty glory. Knowing this helps us to keep going – we can persevere. We can even rejoice.

## To think about

- How does knowing that my present grief and sufferings are achieving a substantial permanent glory for me change how I feel about the situation here and now?
- How does it help me to keep going?

## A prayer

Dear loving Father in Heaven, thank you that when I suffer this is not just meaningless or pointless. Thank you that you are achieving something through it. In fact, you are achieving something great and glorious through it. Please help me, knowing this, to keep going today – to persevere. I ask this in the name of my Lord and Saviour, Jesus Christ. Amen.

# 23. 'All things... for good...'

## The Bible

Read Romans 8:18-30

*... in all things God works for the good of those who love him, who have been called according to his purpose.* (v28)

We have seen that suffering does something to us – it changes us. Even though it is not what we would choose, God uses it.

In Romans 8:28, Paul says that in everything, God is at work for the good of those who love him. This does not mean everything that happens to us is good in itself – it obviously is not. However, it does mean God can and does bring good out of everything that happens to us, even those things that are sad and bad. However, the good that God has in view is a very specific good. It is not just that we will be happy and successful here and now.

Paul spells this out in the next verse: '*For God knew his people in advance, and he chose them to become like his Son, so that his Son would be the firstborn among many brothers and sisters.*'

The good that God is working for is that we should become more like Jesus.

We often hear people quote Romans 8:28. We see it on posters and wall texts. But we should never quote it without also quoting verse 29, to give it this essential context – the 'good' in verse 28 is defined in verse 29 as becoming more like Jesus. This may help to make some sense of our grief and suffering.

As Elisabeth Elliot says, '*He will not necessarily protect us – not from anything it takes to make us more like Jesus.*'[15]

Grief and suffering are making us ready for our future glory by making us more like Christ.

## To think about

- Does knowing that God will use my grief and suffering to make me more like Jesus help me to face it?
- How would my attitude change if I were to reflect more on this?

## A prayer

Dear loving Father in Heaven, thank you that you are always at work in the things that happen to me, even the sad and sorrowful things. Thank you that you use the circumstances of my life to make me more like your Son. Please help me to trust you when I do not understand, and to grow more like Jesus day by day. I pray this in the name of my Lord and Saviour, Jesus Christ. Amen.

*'One day very soon, much sooner than we think, God will close the curtain on sin, sweeping suffering and all its pain and tears away forever. Until that time, He permits what He hates to accomplish something mysterious and wonderful which He loves: Christ in us.'*[16]

- Joni Eareckson Tada

# 24. Fixing our eyes on what we cannot see

## The Bible

Read 2 Corinthians 4:16-18

*Therefore we fix our eyes not on what is seen but on what is unseen. For what is seen is temporary. What is unseen is eternal.* (v18)

We have seen previously that grief and suffering are 'light and momentary', as Paul says. They are only brief, even though it does not feel at all like that while we are caught up in the middle of them.

We have also seen that suffering and grief are actually achieving something in God's purposes. God is using them to change us – to make us more like Christ.

We may believe these things but still feel they are not helping us as much as they should. This leads into the last important thing Paul says in 2 Corinthians 4:18:

*'Therefore we fix our eyes not on what is seen but on what is unseen. For what is seen is temporary. What is unseen is eternal.'*

We fix our eyes on... *what?* On what we cannot see. This sounds like a paradox. How can we fix our eyes on something we cannot see? But Paul is using 'fixing our eyes' as a striking metaphor for giving our full attention to the hope that we cannot yet see.

In times of distress and grief, it's even more important that we fix our attention on our future hope, which we do not yet see, rather than on our present troubles and trials, which we cannot help seeing. We need to spend time thinking about it; we need to dwell on it.

Of course, this is not easy. By definition, what we can see is always right there in front of us. We cannot see our future hope. The problem is not just that we cannot see it, but that the Bible tells us very little about what it is actually like, so we find it difficult to visualise.

At the centre of our hope for the future is the certainty that we shall be with Jesus. In Philippians 1:23, Paul says, '*I long to go and be with Christ, which would be far better for me.*' (New Living Translation)

We need to focus our hopes and our thoughts on being with Christ, rather than worrying too much about what the new creation will be like, or what we will be like in that new creation.

As we said earlier, fixing our attention on our future hope like this is not something that 'just happens'. It takes a deliberate choice – an act of will. And this is not a battle that we just fight once – it is an ongoing struggle. We have to train ourselves to it – and the way we do this (like learning anything) is by making this choice over and over again.

## To think about

- How will fixing my attention on my future hope help me?
- What will help me in practice to fix my eyes on my unseen hope?
- How can I make the choice to do this over and over again?

## A prayer

Dear loving Father in Heaven, thank you that what I can see is only temporary, and that in Christ I have a hope I cannot yet see, which is permanent. Please help me to fix my eyes on this hope – to give it my full attention and to spend time thinking about it. Help me to make a deliberate choice to do this, and to do it over and over again, as often as I need to. I pray this in the name of my Lord and Saviour, Jesus Christ. Amen.

# 25. The past: be thankful

## The Bible

Read Colossians 3:15-17

*And whatever you do, whether in word or deed, do it all in the name of the Lord Jesus, giving thanks to God the Father through him.* (v17)

We should be developing an attitude of hope towards the future. What attitude should we aim to develop towards the past? One danger is that we want to 'live in the past'. Another is that we can become bitter. Nostalgia is toxic and can easily turn into bitterness. The antidote to both of these is to be thankful.

The Bible has a lot to say about being thankful. In Colossians 3:15-17, Paul talks about being thankful (v15); having gratitude in your hearts (v16); and giving thanks (v17). In Colossians 4:2, he says: *'Devote yourselves to prayer, being watchful and thankful.'* And in 1 Thessalonians 5:17, he says: *'Be joyful always; pray continually; give thanks in all circumstances, for this is God's will for you in Christ Jesus.'*

However, when we are going through grief and loss, this can feel hard – perhaps even impossible. Just as we saw when we were thinking about hope for the future, it also takes an act of will to be thankful for the good that we have had, rather than allowing ourselves to live in the past or to become bitter over the good that we have lost. It takes a deliberate choice to respond with gratitude rather than bitterness.

This is not a one-off choice. We have to train ourselves to be thankful, and the way we do this is by doing it over and over again. At first this feels very unnatural, but the more we do it, the more familiar it will feel, until eventually it will become a habit.

## To think about

- What is there in my life today that I am thankful for?
- What practical step can I take to help me be thankful for the good things in my life?

## A prayer

Dear loving Father in Heaven, thank you for all the many good things you have given me. Please help me not to want to live in the past, and not to become bitter, but to choose to be thankful, and to make this choice over and over again until it becomes a habit. I pray this in the name of my Lord and Saviour, Jesus Christ. Amen.

# 26: The present: trust God

## The Bible

Read Philippians 4:4-9

*Do not be anxious about anything, but in every situation, by prayer and petition, with thanksgiving, present your requests to God. And the peace of God, which transcends all understanding, will guard your hearts and your minds in Christ Jesus.* (v6-7)

The world can be a very frightening place. Our instinctive response is to be anxious and fearful. This is amplified in all kinds of ways when we are grieving and distressed. We start to wonder: is God good? Does he really care? Is he in control? In fact, is he really there at all?

If the attitude we need towards the future is hope, and towards the past is thankfulness, the attitude we need towards the present is to trust God.

It is easy to say this, but what exactly does it look like? Trusting God seems straightforward, until something happens that challenges us and makes us think about it more deeply.

First of all, it does not mean we are confident that God will give us whatever particular outcome we are hoping for and praying for. He never guarantees that.

It also does not mean we understand what God is doing. We always want to understand what is going on, and sometimes we can persuade ourselves that we do understand. But we most need to trust God when we do not understand what is happening and we are not happy about it. If we understood, we would not need to trust.

Think about the story of Job: although the book tells *us* why Job suffered, Job himself never found out. Instead, at the end of the book, he was challenged by a new vision of God's greatness – challenged to trust God even when he did not understand.

Rather, trusting God means being confident that he is there, that he is good, that he loves us and cares what happens to us, and that he in control, and then praying on this basis. The result of this kind of praying, according to Paul in Philippians, is that we will have peace – peace from God, which is beyond understanding.

How can we do this?

When fear and anxiety surge up in our hearts, the first place we should look is not at our current circumstances (however distressing they are), but at the cross: at Jesus dying in our place, because this is where we see God's love for us most clearly:

*'God demonstrates his own love for us in this: While we were still sinners, Christ died for us.'* (Romans 5:8)

*'... the Son of God who loved me and gave himself for me.'* (Galatians 2:20)

Then we should bring it to God in prayer: '*Cast all your anxiety on him because you matter to him.*' (1 Peter 5:7, author's translation)

Like the other attitudes we have talked about (hope and thankfulness), we have to choose to trust God, whatever the particular circumstances that are causing us fear and anxiety, and we must make this choice over and over again, until it becomes a habit.

## To think about

- What am I anxious about today?
- What will help me today to see more clearly that God is there, that he is in control of everything that happens, and that I matter to him?
- What will help me develop the habit of trusting God when I do not understand what is happening?

## A prayer

Dear loving Father in Heaven, thank you that you really are there, that you are in control, and that I matter to you. Thank you that I can trust you, even when I do not understand what is happening and do not feel happy about it. Please help me not to be anxious and fearful, but to bring my fears and anxieties to you in prayer, and to know your peace guarding my heart and mind in Christ Jesus. I pray this in the name of my Lord and Saviour, Jesus Christ. Amen.

# Attitudes – what have we discovered?

As followers of Christ, we need to develop the attitude of hope, looking forward to the future day when we shall be with Christ, and God will make all things new; when there will be no more death or mourning or crying or pain. We must grasp the reality that our present troubles are 'light and momentary', but our future glory will be weighty and eternal. Meanwhile, our griefs and trials are actually achieving something for us: God is using them to make us more like Jesus Christ. So we need to fix our eyes on our unseen future hope.

Rather than wanting to live in the past and sinking into nostalgia, we should develop the attitude of thankfulness for all the good in our lives.

For the present, we need to develop the attitude of trusting God and focussing on his love for us. We see this love most clearly in Jesus's death for us.

These attitudes – hope, thankfulness, and trust – do not come naturally to us. We have to make a deliberate choice to develop them. These are not choices that we can make once, and they are settled for the rest of our lives. Rather, we must train ourselves by making these choices over and over again, until they become habits.

# Lamenting together

# 27. Lamenting together

## The Bible

Read Psalm 79:1-13

*Do not hold against us the sins of past generations;*
*may your mercy come quickly to meet us,*
*for we are in desperate need.*
*Help us, God our Saviour,*
*for the glory of your name;*
*deliver us and forgive our sins*
*for your name's sake.*
*Why should the nations say,*
*'Where is their God?'* (v8-10)

Up to this point, we have been thinking about how we discover lament as individuals living broken and messed up lives in a broken and messed up world.

However, we also need to discover how to lament together, in our families and churches.

At the start of these reflections, we said that one reason we need to discover how to lament is that the church today does not seem to know how to handle grief and loss.

However, lamenting together was an accepted part of life in ancient Israel, and forms an important strand in the Bible.

Several of the psalms are *communal* laments, like Psalm 79. (Of course, the book of Psalms is Israel's 'hymn book'. There is a sense in which all the psalms were intended for the community to sing.) These communal lament psalms particularly express the grief and loss of the whole community.

The nation may have suffered a military defeat, or a natural disaster such as a plague. They took these things as signs of God's judgment, and one theme of the communal laments is recognising the community's sin.

Today, we might think of what happens to a community where there has been a major accident, or a natural disaster, or the devastation of war.

Part of how we learn to lament is by discovering again how to lament *together*. The communal lament psalms are both an encouragement for us to do this, and 'worked examples' or models for us of how to do it. Some of the other communal lament psalms are psalms 12, 44, 60, 74, 80, 85, and 90.

## To think about

- What circumstances today might cause my church community to lament together?
- How could my church begin to express its lament as a community?

## A prayer

Dear loving Father in Heaven, thank you that the communal lament psalms are in the Bible. Thank you that they encourage us to lament together and give us examples of how to lament together. Please help us in our families and churches and other groups to learn how to lament together. I pray this in the name of my Lord and Saviour, Jesus Christ. Amen.

# 28. Find a friend

## The Bible

Read Job 2:11-13

*Then they sat on the ground with him for seven days and seven nights. No one said a word to him, because they saw how great his suffering was.* (v13)

We have seen previously that when we are discovering lament, we need to be honest with ourselves and honest with God. We also need to be honest with other people – not to put on a performance that says everything is OK, when it really is not.

It is good to be honest, but it is not necessarily good to open up to the same extent with everyone. We need to choose carefully who we are most open with. Not everyone is equally helpful. When we are going through grief and distress, some people can be quite toxic (think of Job's 'friends'). These people will just drain us spiritually, and it is better to avoid saying too much to them.

Especially unhelpful are the people who want us to 'get over it' or who want to fix us quickly, perhaps by bombarding us with Bible verses or with their theological insights.

However, having acknowledged that some people can be toxic, it is worth trying to find people – or at least one person – who will sit with us in sympathy without rushing in to fix us. The best thing that Job's friends did was to sit with him for seven days without saying anything. It was only when they started to talk that they became toxic.

When we are discovering lament, we need friends – but we need to choose our friends carefully.

## To think about

- Who do I know who could come alongside me without rushing to fix me?
- What do I most hope for from them?

## A prayer

Dear loving Father in Heaven, thank you that you give us friends who understand how we are feeling and who will sit with us in sympathy, without hurrying to fix us. Please give me at least one such friend, and help me to be honest with him or her. I pray this in the name of my Lord and Saviour, Jesus Christ. Amen.

# 29. Be a friend

## The Bible

Read 2 Corinthians 1:3-7

*... the Father of compassion and the God of all comfort, who comforts us in all our troubles, so that we can comfort those in any trouble with the comfort we ourselves receive from God.* (v3-4)

In just two verses, the English version of 2 Corinthians 1 uses the word 'comfort' four times. In the original Greek, Paul uses variations on the same root word five times. The word is *paraklesis*. Its basic meaning is 'to be called alongside' someone. It is sometimes also used with the meaning of 'to encourage' someone.

Paul says here that God comforts us in all our troubles. And one of the reasons God comforts *us* is so that we in turn can comfort *others*, by sharing with them the comfort we have received from him.

Perhaps there is someone in your family, or circle of friends, or church, who is going through grief and distress, whom you could come alongside to help and encourage? Through God helping you, is he equipping you to help them?

In Romans 12:15, Paul says we should '*Rejoice with those who rejoice; mourn with those who mourn.*' What would this look like in practice? Most simply, it would mean spending time with them, being present with them, and sharing in their grief and distress. Based on all we have seen so far, it would not mean rushing in to fix them, or bombarding them with Bible verses or theological insights.

## To think about

- Is there someone I know who is going through distress and grief, whom I could come alongside to encourage and comfort?
- What practical step could I take to do this?

## A prayer

Dear loving Father in Heaven, thank you for the ways you have comforted me in my troubles. Please help me to share the comfort I have received from you with others I know who are also facing troubles. I pray this in the name of my Lord and Saviour, Jesus Christ. Amen.

# 30. Do not give up on the church!

## The Bible

Read 1 Corinthians 12:12-21

*… God has placed the parts in the body, every one of them, just as he wanted them to be. If they were all one part, where would the body be? As it is, there are many parts, but one body. The eye cannot say to the hand, 'I don't need you!' And the head cannot say to the feet, 'I don't need you!'* (v18-21)

When we are facing loss and grief and distress, there will be times when we are tempted to give up on the church. We may feel that no-one understands us, or even that no-one cares very much.

However, it is vitally important to stay involved, and not to give up. We need to stay involved both for our own good and for the good of the whole community.

God has arranged things so that we need each other. As Paul says: *'The eye cannot say to the hand, 'I don't need you!' And the head cannot say to the feet, 'I don't need you.' ... If one part suffers, every part suffers with it; if one part is honoured, every part rejoices with it. Now you are the body of Christ, and each one of you is a part of it.'* (1 Corinthians 12:21, 26-27)

As the writer to the Hebrews puts it: '... *Let us not neglect our meeting together, as some people do, but encourage one another, especially now that the day of his return is drawing near.'* (Hebrews 10:25, New Living Translation)

So even when you feel like you are not achieving anything, you are not getting much out of it, and no-one understands or cares – stay involved and keep going!

## To think about

- How do I feel right now about my church?
- Is there something I could do to change how I feel?

## A prayer

Dear loving Father in Heaven, thank you that you have arranged things in such a way that your body, the church, needs me to play my part, and I need your body, the church. Help me not to give up on the church, but to stay involved and to keep going. I pray this in the name of my Lord and Saviour, Jesus Christ. Amen.

# 31. Leading the church in lament

## The Bible

Read Romans 12:9-16

*Rejoice with those who rejoice; mourn with those who mourn.* (v15)

If you have a leadership role – for example, if you are responsible for pastoring a congregation, for preaching or teaching, or for leading worship, please think and pray regularly and deeply about the people in your congregation who are grieving, who are struggling, for whom everything is not wonderful and positive. How can you help them? (Not by encouraging them to pretend that everything is fine!) How can you be more intentional about making a place for lament in your community's worship and teaching?

One obvious step would be to include some of the lament psalms regularly in your worship.

Another is to think carefully about the worship songs and hymns that you choose. Some songs are much more honest than others about the grief and distress in life.

Another possibility is to preach regularly on some of the 'difficult' parts of the Bible – the lament psalms, or the books of Job or Lamentations.

Whatever you are preaching and teaching about, please be honest about the struggles and difficulties that we face, and do not gloss over them. And if you are not a leader at all, please pray for the leaders you know, that they will learn how to lead the church in lament.

## To think about

- What leadership role – if any – do I have in the church?
- What would it look like for me to be more intentional about including lament in this role?

- What is one practical step I could take to include lament in the life of the church?

## A prayer

Dear loving Father in Heaven, thank you for the opportunities you give me to serve you and your people in my local church. Please help me to be mindful of those who are suffering, and to take deliberate steps to include lament in my service and leadership. I pray, too, for all the people I know who have any kind of leadership role, that you will help them learn how to lead the church in lament. I pray this in the name of my Lord and Saviour, Jesus Christ. Amen.

# Lamenting together – what have we discovered?

We are not meant to lament on our own! In this final section we have been thinking about lamenting with other people. The communal lament psalms are an encouragement to do this. They are 'worked examples' or models of how to do it.

We need to find friends – or at least one friend – who will sit with us in sympathy without rushing in to fix us. We also need to consider whether, through our own grief and distress, God is equipping us to be that kind of friend to someone else who is in distress.

It is important for us to stay involved with our church, and not to give up – we need each other!

If we have a leadership role in church, it is especially important that we think through the place of lament, whether in leading worship or in preaching and teaching.

# Putting it all together

What have we discovered about lament? To lament means to express our grief and distress. For the follower of Jesus Christ, it means expressing our grief and distress to God. It grows out of the tension between believing that God is good and experiencing pain and loss. There is a lot of lament in the Bible, but today we are not familiar with it, which is one reason why we need to discover how to lament.

We begin to discover how to lament when we are honest with ourselves about what we are feeling. We also need to be honest with God – to tell him what we are really thinking and feeling, not what we believe we ought to be thinking and feeling.

The Bible helps us here: people in the Bible were honest with God about how they felt – and God did not condemn them for it. Passages such as the lament psalms and the book of Lamentations give us permission to be honest with God, and they give us words to use when we cannot find the words of our own.

Today, because of the life, death, and resurrection of Jesus Christ, we are in a better place than the writers of Lamentations and the lament psalms. Because Jesus is a man, as well as the Son of God, he understands first-hand what it is like to grieve and to be distressed. He is '*a man of sorrows, acquainted with deepest grief*'. Not only that, but '*He took up our pain, and bore our suffering.*' Today he is in Heaven praying for us. All this is a great encouragement to us when we face loss and grief.

As followers of Christ, there are attitudes we can develop that will help us discover how to lament well – attitudes to the future, to the past, and to the present. For the future, we need to develop the attitude of hope, looking forward to the day when we shall be with Christ; when God will make all things new, and there will be no more death, or mourning, or crying, or pain.

For the past, rather than sinking into nostalgia, we should cultivate the attitude of thankfulness for all the good in our lives. For the present, we need to cultivate the attitude of trusting God and focussing on his love for us. We see this love most clearly in Jesus's death for us.

These attitudes – hope, thankfulness and trust, do not come naturally to us. We have to choose to develop them. This is not a choice that we can make once, and it is settled for the rest of our lives. Rather, we have to train ourselves by making this choice over and over again, until it becomes a habit.

We also need to discover how to lament with other people. The communal lament psalms encourage us to lament together, and they give us 'worked examples' of how to do this.

We need friends who will sit with us in sympathy without rushing in to fix us. We also need to consider whether, through our own grief and distress, God is equipping us to be friends to others who are in distress.

Finally, it is important for us to stay involved with our church, and not to give up – we need each other! If we have a leadership role in church, it is especially important that we think through the place of lament, whether in leading worship or in preaching and teaching.

# Appendix: How is *Lamentations* organised?

There are some hints in the way Lamentations is organised that help us understand its message. Unfortunately, these hints are not obvious in our English translations:

## 1. An A to Z of suffering

Each chapter has 22 verses (except chapter 3 – see the next point). There are 22 letters in the Hebrew alphabet. In the original language, each verse of chapters 1, 2 and 4 begins with a successive letter of the alphabet. It is as if the writer is saying, 'This is an A to Z of suffering. It covers the ground completely, from beginning to end.'

## 2. God's love is central

There are five laments. Chapter 3 is the central one. Today we often put the most important point we are making either at the beginning or the end of something. But ancient writers often arranged things so that the most important point came in the middle.

In our English translations, chapter 3 has 66 verses (i.e. 3 x 22). This might leave us thinking it is three times as long as chapters 1 and 2, but in fact, in chapters 1 and 2, each verse has three lines, while in chapter 3, each verse only has one line. So chapter 3 is the same length as chapters 1 and 2.

Chapter 3 follows the same alphabetic structure as chapters 1 and 2, but each letter of the alphabet gets three verses – AAA, BBB, CCC and so on. (Our translations do not show this.) This is another way the arrangement focuses our attention more intensely on chapter 3.

Chapter 3 is the heart of the message of Lamentations, and at the heart of chapter 3, in verses 21-24, is God's love and compassion and faithfulness: despite everything that has happened, *we are still here*. As the New Living Translation footnote to verse 22 says, 'The faithful love of the Lord keeps us from destruction.'

## 3. The organisation is not perfect – there is no resolution

At a number of points, the careful arrangement breaks down. For example:

Chapter 4 only has two lines per verse, and chapter 5 only has one line per verse. This creates a structure that 'tails off' towards the end of Lamentations.

In chapter 5, although there are 22 verses, they do not follow an alphabetical order like the other chapters.

The alphabetical order is not perfect – In chapters 2, 3, and 4, the verse beginning with the letter *pe* (the 17th letter of the Hebrew alphabet) comes before the verse beginning with *ayin* (the 16th letter). These verses are 'out of order'.

Is it just that the writer could not be bothered to arrange things properly? Or is there some deliberate purpose behind these ways the structure breaks down?

Lamentations has been very carefully crafted. The writer is not just 'letting it all hang out'.

The imperfect arrangement says to us that life is not perfectly organised and sorted out. Sometimes it is messy and ambiguous. Yes, God is good and faithful and merciful, but there is still pain and loss, and – for the time being – the tension remains. There is no resolution, and Lamentations ends with a prayer, on a note of uncertainty: '... *unless you have utterly rejected us and are angry with us beyond measure.*' (5:22)

# Further reading

Kenneth Boa and Jenny Abel, *Shaped by Suffering: How Temporary Hardships Prepare us for our Eternal Home*, IVP, 2020

Joni Eareckson Tada, *A Place of Healing: Wrestling with the Mysteries of Suffering, Pain, and God's Sovereignty,* David C Cook, 2010

Janine Fair, *Surprised by Grief: A Journey into Hope*, IVP, 2010

Eric Gaudion, *Braving the Storm: Survival Tactics*, Authentic Media, 2007

Eric Gaudion, *Storm Force: Winning the Battle for the Mind*, Authentic Media, 2009

Eric Gaudion, *Through the Storms: A Manual for when Life Hurts*, Instant Apostle, 2020

Douglas Groothuis, *Walking Through Twilight: A Wife's Illness – a Philosopher's Lament,* IVP, 2017

Timothy Keller, *Walking with God through Pain and Suffering*, Hodder & Stoughton, 2013

C. S. Lewis, *A Grief Observed*, Faber & Faber, 2013

Paul Mallard, *Learning to Lament: Our Heavenly Father's Embrace when we Grieve*, Union Publishing, 2023

Mark Meynell, *When Darkness Seems My Closest Friend: Reflections on Life and Ministry with Depression*, IVP, 2018

Matt Searles, *Tumbling Sky: Psalm Devotions for Weary Souls*, 10Publishing, 2017

David W. Smith, *Stumbling Toward Zion: Recovering the Biblical Tradition of Lament in the Era of World Christianity*, Langham Global Library, 2020

Federico G. Villaneuva, *It's OK to be not OK: Preaching the Lament Psalms*, Langham Preaching Resources, 2017

Mark Vroegop, *Dark Clouds, Deep Mercy: Discovering the Grace of Lament*, Crossway, 2019

Kristen Wetherell and Sarah Walton, *Hope When It Hurts: Biblical Reflections to help you Grasp God's Purpose in your Suffering*, The Good Book Company, 2017

# Endnotes

[1] Taken from *Dark Clouds, Deep Mercy* by Mark Vroegop, p. 26. Copyright © 2019, Used by permission of Crossway, a publishing ministry of Good News Publishers, Wheaton, IL 60187, *www.crossway.org*.

[2] Taken from *The God I don't understand: reflections on tough questions of faith,* by Christopher J H Wright, p. 53. Copyright © 2008. Used by permission of HarperCollins Christian Publishing. *www.harpercollinschristian.com*

[3] Taken from *The God I don't understand: reflections on tough questions of faith,* by Christopher J H Wright, p. 52. Copyright © 2008. Used by permission of HarperCollins Christian Publishing. *www.harpercollinschristian.com*

[4] Federico G. Villanueva, *It's OK to be Not OK: Preaching the Lament Psalms,* Langham Preaching Resources, 2017. *langhamliterature.org*

[5] Taken from *Letters of John Newton,* p. 180. Copyright © 1960. Used by permission of Banner of Truth. *banneroftruth.org/uk*

[6] Taken from *The God I don't understand: reflections on tough questions of faith,* by Christopher J H Wright, p. 52. Copyright © 2008. Used by permission of HarperCollins Christian Publishing. *www.harpercollinschristian.com*

[7] Taken from *Tumbling Sky,* by Matt Searles, pp. 20-21. Copyright © 2017. Used by permission of 10Publishing. *uk.10ofthose.com/departments/10-publishing*

[8] Taken from *Until He Looks Down and Sees: the Message and Meaning of the Book of Lamentations,* by Heath

Thomas, p. 4. Copyright © 2009. Used by permission of Grove Books, *www.grovebooks.co.uk*.

[9] Taken from *Doubt: Faith in two minds,* by Os Guinness, p. 222. Copyright © 1976. Used by permission of SPCK. *spckpublishing.co.uk*

[10] Taken from *Expositor's Bible Commentary volume 6, Lamentations,* by H. L. Ellison, p. 699. Copyright © 1986. Used by permission of HarperCollins Christian Publishing. *www.harpercollinschristian.com*

[11] Taken from *The Cross of Christ,* by John Stott, p. 335-336. Copyright © 2006. Used by permission of SPCK. *spckpublishing.co.uk*

[12] Taken from *Dark Clouds, Deep Mercy* by Mark Vroegop, p. 66. Copyright © 2019. Used by permission of Crossway, a publishing ministry of Good News Publishers, Wheaton, IL 60187, *www.crossway.org*.

[13] From a letter to Mary Willis Shelburne on June 17th, 1963, in *C S Lewis Collected Letters Volume 3*, edited by Walter Hooper. Copyright © 2006. Used by permission of HarperCollins Christian Publishing. *www.harpercollinschristian.com*

[14] Taken from *Finishing Our Course With Joy* by J. I. Packer, p. 23. Copyright © 2014. Used by permission of Crossway, a publishing ministry of Good News Publishers, Wheaton, IL 60187, *www.crossway.org*.

[15] Taken from *Be Still My Soul,* by Elisabeth Elliot, p. 48. Copyright © 2004. Used by permission of Baker Publishing Group, *bakerpublishinggroup.com*

Printed in Great Britain
by Amazon